Japanese Heraldry

Thomas R. H. McClatchie

JAPANESE HERALDRY,

BY

THOMAS R. H. McCLATCHIE,

H. B. M.'s CONSULAR SERVICE, JAPAN.

Read before the Asiatic Society of Japan, on the
25th October, 1876.

———o———

In almost every land where feudalism has existed, Heraldry has enjoyed distinguished honour and careful attention. The annals of every European country, at least, will show conclusively that the " nobyl and gentyl sciaunce," as old Heralds delighted to term it, has become so bound up and intimately connected with History, that the two are hardly separable. Although the fanciful symbols of Heraldry have not as yet been regarded in Eastern climes with the same amount of consideration as amongst the nations of the West, it is nevertheless well known that the germs of the science exist, and perhaps have only lacked the fostering influence of advancing civilization in order to attain to a full growth. Japan, where the feudal system has flourished for an extraordinarily lengthy period, is no exception to this rule, and it is of Japanese Heraldry that this paper proposes to treat.

In comparing Japanese with European Heraldry, it will, as might naturally be expected, at once be seen that the former is remarkably deficient in rule, variety of style, and general character of treatment. So meagre, indeed, is it that it can hardly be deemed worthy of comparison except with the very earliest Heraldry of the West. It is allowed by Heralds that before the adoption of regular coats-of-arms there existed in Europe merely what were termed Badges, that is, "figures or devices assumed for "the purpose of being borne either absolutely alone, or "in connection with a Motto, as the distinctive cognizance "of an individual or a family." Up to the present time Japanese Heraldry has advanced no father than this primary state. No such thing as a coat-of-arms proper has ever been known in the country, and the only distinctive marks hitherto in use have been Badges and Crests. This is, in a great degree, owing to the fact that the shield, on which in Europe the arms of the bearer were blazoned, has never been in vogue in Japan. The only piece of defensive armour at all resembling it used in Japanese warfare was a large screen of wood, fixed in an upright position by a moveable rest at the back, so as to form a protection for archers. The smaller shield for the arm would have proved a serious encumbrance to a warrior, as the long Japanese sword is two-handed. Thus, then, the only place where the distinguishing mark could be borne was either on the helmet or on the breast-plate, and in this way crests and badges are the only Heraldic insignia here known. The deficiency, however, has partly been remedied by the frequent instances of these devices being marked upon flags or banners of different colours, and it is a curious fact that a large number of these flags could be accurately described by any European Heraldic scholar, in the set phraseology peculiar to his art, so that the shape, colour, etc., of the flag and the device could be correctly delineated from the mere written details. But as a general rule the Japanese do not adhere to those strict laws regarding the combination of metals and tinctures observed in Western lands; they care but little how often the colour of their symbols may be altered, provided only that the general outline of the device be preserved; and this alone is quite sufficient to show that their system of Heraldry is as yet far from perfect. In spite, however, of their deficiency in regard to these most essential points, they still possess various rough laws and are guided by certain usages which show that there exist, without doubt, the rudiments of a system that may eventually be matured into something approaching more closely to regular Heraldic art.

How and when Badges first came into use in Japan is a matter enveloped in considerable obscurity. The popular tradition seems to be that they took their origin from the patterns embroidered upon, or woven into, the state garments of the old court nobles at Kiyôto, and in support of this theory there is adduced the fact that the Chinese character used in writing to express the word Badge or Crest (no distinction being made between the two) is a compound of two other characters signifying "thread-pattern" or "thread-writing." The embroidered patterns alluded to were generally circular, and hence it comes to pass that nearly all Japanese Heraldic devices are more or less circular in shape. At the very first, a difference was made in the size of the Badge, according to the rank of the wearer. Those of nobles and officials of high position were no less than three inches in diameter, while subordinate officers and persons of lower rank used smaller ones, down to the ordinary gentry, in whose case the diameter was but one inch in length. In latter times, however, the Badges were very seldom borne larger than the size last-mentioned, except when blazoned on flags or on breastplates. A miniature facsimile of the Badge was generally worn on the helmet as well, being placed in the front, and often between the horns of a crescent shaped piece of metal called *tatémono*, used as an ornament thereon. Thus it would appear that the Japanese owned no distinction between a Crest and a Badge. According to the colour of the flag or the breastplate, so did the tincture of the device vary. On a dark-coloured ground it would be blazoned in gold, white, or red ; while on a lighter ground, black or red were generally used. Sometimes families of rank assumed to themselves, as a kind of livery, a special colour for their banners or war-surcoats. The "Nihon Gu'aishi," a standard history of Japan, states with regard to Taira no Takamochi that " his

" descendants for generations were military vassals (of
" the Crown). They used a red flag." And again,
speaking of Minamoto no Tsunémoto, it is remarked in the
same work that " his descendants were military vassals
" from generation to generation, and they used a white
" flag." The two warriors to whom allusion is here made
lived in the early part of the 10th century, and were the
founders of the two rival families of *Hei* and *Gen*, or
Taira and *Minamoto* ; and these colours were constantly
displayed, in after years, in civil conflicts that caused as
much bloodshed as the English wars of the Red and White
Roses. It is, too, a well known fact that these two
families had also their distinctive cognizances, and the
Badges of many of their chief retainers have likewise
been handed down to posterity, so that it would appear
to be a perfectly reasonable conjecture that a kind of rude
Heraldry had existed in Japan far earlier than the year
900 A.D.

In Japan, as in European countries, the badges were at
first assumed at will by anyone wishing to select for himself and his family some distinguishing mark. In later
times, apart from such assumption, there are to be found
instances of badges being conferred by a chieftain upon
such of his retainers as had distinguished themselves by
bravery in fight or by some other deed of merit. As a
general rule, however, each man selected his own, and
this custom has continued until the present date, so that
it is by no means uncommon to see members of the same
family wearing different badges. A good instance of a
badge being " conferred " is to be found in the history of
the family of Kumagae Naozané, one of the chief-retain-
ers of the Minamoto clan. At the battle of Ishibashiyama,
near Hakoné, in 1181 A.D., Minamoto no Yoritomo was
signally defeated by the Taira forces, and fled away,
hotly pursued, accompanied by only two or three of his
followers. He concealed himself in a hollow tree on
the mountain, to avoid the enemy's scouts, and it is said
that one of the latter actually thrust his bow inside
the tree to ascertain if any one were hiding within it.

It is narrated in the "Gempei Sei-sui-ki," or "History of the rise and fall of the Gen and Hei," that "the bow touched the sleeve of Yoritomo's coat of "mail, whereupon he prayed fervently to Hachiman (the " god of war), when as if for a sign, there flew forth from "the hollow tree two wood-pigeons, clapping their wings "loudly." The pursuers, on seeing the birds, gave up the idea that anyone could be concealed in the tree, and a heavy shower of rain coming on at the moment they abandoned the pursuit. The guide-book to the Nakasendô says, in speaking of the town of Kumagaë,—the residence of Naōzané,—through which that road passes, that "as a reward for his (Naōzané's) services at the "battle of Ishibashiyama, when he concealed Yori-"tomo in a fallen tree, he received from the latter a "curtain marked with the mistletoe and pigeon "badges." It may be mentioned in this connection that a badge so conferred was not always worn by the recipient in preference to the one which might already be possessed by himself; but could be used at option either as the real or second badge. As an instance of the "assumption " of a badge, there may be quoted the origin of that borne by the family of Niwa, holding one of the Northern daimiates. It is said that an ancestor of this family once went out to battle, bearing as a distinctive mark what was termed a *sashimono*, that is, a small rod, fastened into a socket at the back of the cuirass, which was usually adorned with a small flag bearing the badge of the wearer suspended from a slender cross-bar fastened at one end to the main staff. That of Niwa, however, was only ornamented with eight thin strips of metal hanging from it. When the fight was over it was found that no less than six of these had been hewn away, while the remaining two were bent one across the other in the form of the letter X., or a "cross saltire,"—and this figure was consequently assumed by Niwa as his family badge. Another version of the tale, however, has it that the warrior in question killed so many of his adversaries that after wiping his sword, according to Japanese custom, upon the left knee of his wide trousers after each several encounter, the stains of blood eventually left upon the garment two broad lines in the shape just described. This latter explanation is given by some of the former retainers of the Niwa family, and therefore is probably the more correct of the two. Again, the badge borne by a family named Narita, formerly adherents of the above-mentioned house of Niwa, represents two parallel lines drawn through a circle, and extending for some distance beyond the circumference. The founder of this family, so the tale runs, was once engaged in one of the frequent wars on the Eastern marches of Japan, and his provisions having failed, was put to great straits to obtain food,—a battle being imminent at the time. Casting his eyes around, he espied in the mountains a small shrine, and entering this, found laid therein as an offering a bowl of rice and a pair of chopsticks. The pangs of hunger overcame any religious scruples that Narita may have possessed ; he seized the bowl and devoured the rice, and refreshed by this timely sustenance, went forth and bore himself gallantly in the fight. In it he earned considerable distinction, and ascribing this to the favour of the deity whose shrine he had invaded, he took for his badge the circle and two lines, as a rough delineation of the rice-bowl and chopsticks. The above quoted instances will suffice to give a general idea of the manner in which crests or badges were conferred or assumed in the ancient days of Japan.

Most of the great nobles, as may be seen by a glance at any Japanese list of *daimiôs*, possessed three badges, whilst those of lower rank had two, and ordinary *samurai* but one, except in some few instances. Of these, one was always termed the *jô-mon* or " fixed badge"of the family, the others being styled *kaë-mon*, or badges worn instead of the chief one, and these were used on occasions when it was not absolutely necessary to appear in full dress. In time of war, the soldiers in Japan always fought in full armour, and then the crest or badge was of course a conspicuous mark whereby to distinguish friend from foe in the battlefield. It was then displayed on the breastplate, the helmet, and the small flag attached to the *sashimono* as mentioned above. It was also marked upon the curtains usually fastened to upright posts so as to form an enclosure around a military encampment. In time of peace, the badge was as now, generally worn in five places on the upper garment, namely, at the back of the neck, on each sleeve, and on each breast. In some instances, however, the number was increased to seven, by the addition of two upon the collar or margin of the garment, just over the chest, and in a line with those on the breasts. Apart from the clothing, nearly every article of common use was marked in like manner. The badge appeared on the lacquered hat, the fittings of the swords or spear-shafts, the *norimono* or planquin, travelling boxes, lanterns, etc., of every Japanese gentleman ; and, in the case of a *daimiô,* these distinguishing marks were noted down with such accuracy in the lists of nobles, that by the insignia of a train or retinue on any of the highroads, the name and the rank of their lord could at once be determined. Of so great importance was this deemed in a country where etiquette required the observance of various details of ceremony when two nobles and their followers met on the road, that there were generally placed in the van of every procession two or three well-informed retainers,—a kind of Heralds, as it were, —whose special duty it was to take note of the insignia of any train coming from an opposite direction, and pass word down their own ranks as to the due ceremony to be observed under the circumstances. These heralds had by no means an easy duty to perform, for they fell into great disgrace if they failed in what was required of them. It was customary in these trains for the whole of the inferior attendants to wear their lord's badge on their mantles, to facilitate recognition by other travellers. On the castle residences of Japanese nobles in the country, and also on their *yashikis* or fortified mansions in Yedo or elsewhere, the badge of the owner was conspicuously displayed. It was placed over the large gateway, the 2nd badges, if such existed, being placed alongside in many cases;—the large tiles at the extremities of the roof-ridge and end beams also were marked with it, and in some cases the whole of the smaller tiles along the edge of the roof were ornamented with the 2nd badge. It was not very usual to place the chief badge on these smaller tiles. If a *Daimiô* changed his residence, these tiles, so marked, were generally removed, but if not, the badge was always carefully erased, the space being left blank if the new occupant did not care to fill it with his own cognizance. Sometimes, as an especial mark of favour, a feudal chieftain would permit one of his retainers, whom he wished to highly honour, to make use of his own badge ; but in such rare instances there was always given to the retainer a *haöri*,—the upper mantle worn by the military class,—marked with the badge, and the privilege lasted only so long as that particular garment was in existence. Nor was the recipient of this favour permitted himself to mark the badge upon any other part of his clothing, and it does not seem that any *hereditary* honour was attached to the gift. From the above remarks it may be be seen that in the case of nobles, at least, there existed some kind of restriction preventing the assumption of a family badge belonging to another house. · No badge was worn by the principal during the ceremony of the *harakiri* ; nor again, at funerals, was any marked on the white mourning garments. At marriage ceremonies, in very high families, neither the bride nor bridegroom wore a badge on their clothing. The regulations as to women's badges have always been rather vague, but as a general custom it would seem that they commonly wore that of their own family, even retaining it after marriage, though then the badge of the husband's family was occasionally taken in preference.

It may here be interesting to note the devices borne by some of the chief families of Japan, as selected from the list of nobles. But firstly the badges of the Imperial line claim our attention. They are two in number. The first is a representation of the *kiku,* or chrysanthemum flower, and is usually delineated by sixteen petals, conjoined, and rounded at the outer extremities, issuing from a small circle in the centre. Some Japanese, however, state that this is not the chrysanthemum, but is intended as a representation of the sun, so as to bear some connection with the red sun on the national flag, of which mention is made below. But this latter theory seems wholly unworthy of credence, as the *kiku* is frequently represented as a *double* flower,—that is, with the rounded extremities of sixteen other petals showing, from below, in the interstices at the ends of those drawn in the foreground. It is, nevertheless, a fact worthy of remark, that in European Heraldry, when the Sun is blazoned as "in his splendour," *i.e.* irradiated, the rays are nearly always *sixteen* in number, though they are then always drawn with *pointed* extremities. The *kiku* is used as a mark on the hilts of the swords forged by the Emperor Go-Toba, who ascended the throne in 1186. The second of the Imperial badges is a representation of the leaf and flower of the *kiri*, or *Paulownia Japonica*, as it is termed in botany; it displays three leaves, and three flowers, each of the latter consisting of a slender stem with the buds attached. The central stem bears seven buds, and those on the sides five each;—thus this badge is termed in Japanese the "*go-shichi no kiri*," or "five and-seven *kiri*." Many other families bear the *kiri* badge, but, as a general rule, the buds are but five in number on the central stem, and three on each of the others,—such a one being styled "*go-san no kiri*," or "five-and-three *kiri*." This law regarding the difference in the number of buds is not, however, observed very strictly. The small square banner usually borne before the Mikado when he drives out in public, bears the *kiku* badge in gold upon a ground of red and gold brocade. Thus allusion is made, in a popular song written at the time of the expedition against Chôshiu in 1866, to the "Imperial Standard of Brocade," and during the troubles in Yedo in 1868, the "loyal troops" earned the nickname of *kingiré* from the *shreds of brocade* which they wore as a distinguishing mark upon the right shoulder. The *kiri* badge, embroidered in gold, is now every day to be seen upon the uniforms of Japanese officials. But, to speak of the badges of some of the nobles. the following short list will suffice as a sample :—

I.—TOKUGAWA, (late *Shôgun*)	Three leaves of the hollyhock, within a circle; the points of the leaves meeting in the centre.
II.—MAEDA, *daimiôs* of Kaga.	A plum-blossom of five petals,—each of circular shape.
III.—SHIMADZU, *daimiôs* of Satsuma.	The ring of a horse's bridle bit.
IV.—YAMANO-UCHI, *daimiôs* of Tosa.	1st.—Three leaves of the *kashiwa* (a kind of oak) within a circle. 2nd.—Two horizontal and parallel lines. 3rd.—The same as the 1st, but without the circle; the stems of the leaves being in each case joined in the centre, the ends pointing outwards.
V.—KURODA, *daimiôs* of Chikuzen.	1st.—A black ball. 2nd.—Three flowers of the *fuji*, or wisteria, conjoined in the centre, and flexed in circular form.
VI.—HACHISUKA, *daimiôs* of Awa, in Shikoku.	1st.—Same as Tokugawa, only of different colour. 2nd.—The figure called a *manji*, within a circle. 3rd.—The same without the circle.
VII.—ARIMA, *daimiôs* of Chikugo.	1st.—The gentian leaves and flowers, arranged in a peculiar circular form. 2nd. – The figure called *mitsu tomoyé*.
VIII.—IKEDA, *daimiôs* of Bizen.	1st.—A butterfly "displayed," or, with wings spread open. 2nd.—Two similar butterflies, fronting each other.
IX.—NAMBU, *daimiôs* of Morioka, in the province of Mutsu.	1st.—Two Cranes, with wings extended, fronting each other, within a circle. 2nd and 3rd.—Four lozenge-shaped figures, arranged so as to form one large lozenge.

X.—Môri, *daimiôs* of Chôshiu.
{
1st.—The leaf and flower of a water-plant called *omodaka*.
2nd & 3rd.—A horizontal line, with three balls, or stars, arranged underneath it in a pyramidical form.
}

XI.—Date, *daimiôs* of Sendai, in the province of Mutsu.
{
1st.—Two sparrows, with wings extended, fronting each other, within two branches of the bamboo arranged in circular form.
2nd.—The peony leaf and flower.
3rd.—A circle, enclosing three perpendicular lines.
}

XII.—Asano, *daimiôs* of Aki.
{
1st.—The feathered ends of two arrows, crossed, within a circle.
3rd.—The same, without the circle.
}

The Tokugawa badge above-mentioned was delineated on flags as either gold or silver upon a blue ground. This badge is stated in the "Nihon Guaishi" to have been adopted by Kiyoyasu, father of the famous Tokugawa Iyéyasu, in the year 1529. Kiyoyasu, returning from a successful expedition against the eastern portion of the province of Mikawa, was entertained by one of his vassals, named Honda Masatada, at the latter's castle of Ina in the above province. During the feast, Honda presented his lord with some food placed on a small wooden stand upon which were laid three leaves of the hollyhock. Kiyoyasu, observing them, exclaimed, "upon my return in triumph "I have received these leaves ; from henceforth I will "adopt them as my badge." A less authentic version of the tale has it that the Tokugawa badge was originally taken from that of the house of Honda, who bore as their cognizance three similar leaves, but with stalks attached and placed perpendicularly within the circle. Iyéyasu, it is said, was once admiring this badge, when Honda Tada-katsu, the son of the above-mentioned Masatada, begged him to adopt it as his own. "I should like to do so, "said "Iyéyasu," but I am sorry (*habakari*) to deprive you "of it." "Then take the *ha bakari* ("the leaves alone")" was Honda's punning retort, " and I will retain "the original badge of both stalks and leaves." Iyéyasu

did so, and thus assumed the modern Tokugawa badge
instead of that previously borne by his family,—a horizontal black line within a white circle.   The "black
ball" of Kuroda was originally a circle within which
were drawn several black cranes. This badge was called
the *sem-ba-dzuru*, or "thousand cranes," but as it was
found to be far too great a labour to depict the birds accurately in each several case, it eventually assumed the
present form. This is the badge displayed in the former
Chikuzen *yashiki* at Yedo, now used as the Department
of Foreign Affairs ;—the Second Badge, the wisteria,
being marked on all the small tiles along the edges of the
roofs of the outer building. The *manji* badge of Awa is
curious. This figure is drawn thus, 卍, and sometimes,
but less frequently, thus, 卐. It is taken from a
Chinese character meaning "ten thousand," and is a
Buddhist symbol, supposed to be emblematical of good
luck. It is frequently to be seen on Buddhist temples,
as a sign of *Fudô Sama*, or the "motionless Buddha."
It was often marked upon the lids of coffins, being supposed to act as a charm to protect the corpse against
the attacks of a demon in the shape of a cat, called
ku'a·ha, which was said to seize and mangle the dead
bodies of human beings. An exact facsimile of this
figure is also to be met with in European Heraldry,
but it is a very rare 'charge.' It is there termed a
"fylfot," but nothing is known as to its origin,—the only
description given in Heraldic works bing that it is "supposed to have been a mystic symbol." The *mitsu-tomoyé*
of Arima, is shaped thus, ◉, being—as its name implies
—a triplicate representation of the single *tomoyé*, ◉.
Many different explanations are given in regard to this
figure. One is that it represents "snow falling whirling
down" (a common expression in Japanese descriptions of
a snow storm),—another, that it is intended to depict
waves dashing up and breaking against a rock,—and a
third that it is a delineation of the *tomo*, or small leathern
glove, consisting of loops for the fingers attached by thin

strips of leather to a broader piece fixed on the back of the hand, as worn in ancient times by Japanese archers. The last of these three would seem to be the explanation most worthy of credence. The *mitsu-tomoyé*, like the *manji*, is also frequently used as a symbol of good-luck, and is to be seen constantly on the small tiles of the *yashikis* in Yedo. As a rule, only the one figure is thus shown, but in some instances it is surrounded by a circle of small balls, varying at times in number. On a gateway in the post-town of Hodogaya, on the Tôkaidô, to the west of Yokohama, appears a device of three single *tomoyé* interlaced. The crossed arrow-feathers of the *daimiôs* of Aki may be found, beautifully carved, on the tomb of Asano Takumi no kami, a cadet of that house, in the cemetery of the temple of Sengakuji in Yedo.

The above are but a few of the badges of the noble families of Japan. Apart from these, there may be observed on all sides exceedingly numerous devices, widely different in style and character. It is, of course, utterly impossible in a short paper to give any details of these, but any one feeling interested in the study of Japanese Heraldic art will find it an easy matter to obtain many curious specimens of badges. In a country gifted like Japan with luxuriant vegetation, it is not surprising that by far the greater number of devices should consist of representations of flowers, leaves, fruits, blossoms, grasses, etc. Amongst these may be mentioned the *kiri* leaf and flower,—the rose (always drawn exactly as in European Heraldry),—the flowering gentian (*sasarindô*), —the chrysanthemum leaf and flower,—the creeping wisteria,—the *kashiwa*,—the holly-hock,—the sorrel leaf,— the peony,—the orange,—the clove,—the pear,—the plum and cherry blossoms,—the bamboo,—and the radish (*daikon*). The animal kingdom is also well represented, though it is a noticeable fact that there do not exist any badges showing portions of the human body, so often to be met with in other countries. Nor, again, are there found many quadrupeds, the solitary instance, at least in the devices of the nobles, being that of a black horse, tethered to two stakes, borne by the family of Sôma, formerly holding a small *daimiate* in the province of Mutsu. There certainly is another figure, termed the *kara-shishi*, which is supposed to represent a lion, but it bears no resemblance whatever to that animal, and so may be set down as a mere fanciful symbol. Birds and insects, however, are favourite subjects. Among these are found cranes, geese, pigeons, sparrows, butterflies, and wasps. The celestial objects worn as badges are the sun, moon, and supposed representations of stars and clouds ; these, however, are very rare. As natural objects, the only two instances are running water, and a mountain-peak. The water is always delineated in conjunction with some other device, as for instance, by the family of Kusunoki, a chrysanthemum flower issuing from a stream of water,—by that of Nakayama, the sun issuing in like manner,—and again, by that of Midzuno, an *omodaka* plant similarly depicted. The only example of a mountain in the list of *daimiôs* is the badge of a small *daimiô* named Aöki Gengorô, formerly lord of the small castle-town of Asada, near Ôsaka, in the province of Setsu, which badge displays a perfect delineation of the summit of Mount Fuji, showing three of the peaks, issuing from clouds. After these come a host of miscellaneous devices, of every possible shape and design,—such as fans (sometimes bearing some smaller charge, and sometimes plain),—the framework only of fans,— ladders,— wheels,—fences,— mallets,— cash,— arrows,— hats,— gateways,— bridle-bits,—Chinese characters, etc., etc. As smaller and simpler designs may be noted circles, lines, squares, hexagons and lozenges, several of these being in some cases conjoined so as to form one badge. In a few instances, very complicated devices are formed by combination of two or more totally different objects, as for instance, three leaves conjoined in the centre and pointing outwards, placed above three others arranged in the form of a triangle, the whole within a circle;—and on one of the small *yashikis* in Banchô, Yedo, there yet remain tiles marked with a strange badge showing one-half of an eight-spoked wheel, between four broad leaves, two on either side,—the whole being enclosed within what appear to be the stalks of some plant bent into circular form.

It is just possible, from this example, that there may have existed in Japan some vague idea of what is termed Heraldic Marshalling, *i.e.*, the combination of two or more Heraldic compositions so as to form one single composition, but there are certainly no definite rules on this important point.

There exists in Japan some crude notion of "differencing" Heraldic devices, that is to say, modifying or adding to the original so as to indicate the difference between two or more families sprung at the first from the same stock. The common system of "differencing" by colour could not be carried out in the ordinary use of Japanese badges, as, when these were worn on clothing, they were always marked in white, but in the case of flags, etc., that admitted of a change in the colour of the grounding, the task was rendered more easy of accomplishment. Thus, the hollyhock badge of the Tokugawa house was marked, in the case of the head family, in gold or silver upon a blue flag, while the kindred houses of Mito, Owari, and Kii, bore each some modification of the same. That of Mito was black on a white flag; Owari's white on a flag striped horizontally white and black; and Kii's, white on a blue ground, the interstices of the leaves being filled in with black, and not allowing the ground colour of the flag to be visible. The delineation of the badge itself was, however, identical in the whole four cases. Other instances might be quoted, but the above is sufficient to illustrate the Japanese idea of "difference."

In Japan, also, as in Europe, there is found many an example of what is termed "Canting Heraldry," consisting of devices which have an allusion to the name of the bearer, thus forming a kind of rebus. One instance is that of a family called Hashimoto, whose badge, the buttresses or "foundation" of a "bridge," gives an exact rendering of the name. The free use of Chinese characters as badges of course gives rise to many opportunities for such punning allusions, and thus we find the families of Ii, Honda, Kuki, Okubo, Inouyé and others, bearing as their cognizances characters the reading of which gives the sound of the first syllable of their name. Again, in the *Hakubutsuku'an*, or Exhibition Department, in Yedo, there is exhibited a beautiful specimen of a *sashimono*, as above described, to which no description is attached, but the badge marked thereon,—a " temple gate-way,"— together with a second device displayed below, serve at once to make known the fact that it belonged to some member of the house of *Torii*, a family formerly holding the daimiate of Mibu, in the province of Shimotsŭké.

Flags and banners of various shapes have been in use in Japan from the earliest ages. They are first mention- ed, in the history called " Nihonki," as having been borne by the army of the Empress Jingô in her expedition against Corea, in 201 A.D. ; and from the year 900 A.D. onwards frequent allusion is made to them in Japanese works. The very earliest kind of standard was the *setsu*, the original insignia of a Commander in Chief, which consisted simply of a bundle of hair from a bull's tail, fastened to the end of a staff. In later times the favourite forms of flags were those called *fuki-nagashi*, and *hata*. The latter of these was an oblong-shaped banner, gene- rally several feet in length and breadth, which was sus- pended from a small cross-bar affixed to the staff ; the *fuki-nagashi* was a smaller edition of this, very narrow, and terminating in two long streamers. In one ·of the shrines at Enoshima there is still shown an old speci- men of a *hata*, said to have belonged to a member of the family of Hôjô, a powerful house that was for a long time a hanger-on of the Minamoto clan, and itself held supremacy in Japan during the 13th and 14th cen- turies. This *hata* is about 5 feet in length by 3 in breadth, and is made of coarse stuff of a blue colour, embroidered with gold. At the top are broidered two *mino-gamé*, or fiery-tailed tortoises, and at the foot a large five clawed dragon. Towards the centre appears the Hôjô badge, consisting of three equilateral triangles arranged in the form of a pyramid, a central space of similar shape being left vacant. This is called the *uroko* badge, supposed to represent a fish's scales, the legend being that Benten-sama, the Sea Goddess worshipped at Enoshima, appeared to Hôjô no Tokimasa (b. 1137—d. 1216) and bestowed this upon him as the cognizance of his family. The narrow *fuki-nagashi* were ordinarily used to mark out the bounds of military encampments, and it was in Japanese warfare a common stratagem to change or alter them so as to deceive the enemy and lure them into an ambuscade. During the civil wars in the period O-nin (1467—1469 A.D.) two brothers of the Hatakéyama family were ranged on opposite sides, and it is narrated in the "Yamato Ji-shi," a small encyclopœdia published in Tenwa (1681—84) that confusion was caused by the fact of their both displaying the same kind of white flag, and that one of the brothers therefore invented and used a different style of flag, called *nobori*. This *nobori* was but an enlarged *sashimono,* as already described, and is now always to be seen on the occasion of a Japanese festival. In recent times, the Japanese have adopted the European style of flag for use on ship board and also in the field.

The national flag of Japan, so well known to every foreigner resident in this country, displays the device of a red ball on a white ground. This red ball is termed in Japannse *hi-no-maru,* or "circle of the sun," in allusion to the fact of Japan being the most distant Eastern country. The adoption of this as the national flag was only notified by the Government in 1859, but the *hi-no-maru* had been for centuries before that time a very favourite badge. At the *Hakubutsu-ku'an* there is to be seen an old standard, described as the "sun and moon standard." This curious specimen consists of a staff, on the end of which is fixed a large white crescent, with the horns upwards, surmounted again by a small red ball: from below the crescent hangs down what appears to be a bunch of white horse-hair. In the 19th volume of a work entitled the " Yedo Meisho Dzuyé," or " Pictorial

Guide to the celebrated localities of Yedo," there is given an illustration of a *sashimono* bearing a precisely similar device. This *sashimono*, it is stated, belonged to one Chiba no Tanémichi who was in charge of the hamlets in the department of Kokubu, Shimôsa, in the period Jiuyei (1182-85). It is possible that the old standard above mentioned may date from about the same period. Prior to this time, the Emperor Takakura (acc. 1169, abd. 1180) presented at the shrine of Itsuku-shima, in the province of Aki, thirty fans, which, as the "Gempei Sei-sui-ki" narrates, "were all pink fans, bearing the *hi-no-maru.*" When Takakura's successor, the Emperor An-toku, was carried away to the West by the Taira family, when they fled from Kiyôto before the Genji forces in 1182, he visited the shrine, when one of these fans was given to him by the priest in charge, who asserted that "the sun thereon was the spirit of the late Emperor,— "and that the arrows of the foe would be caused by it to "recoil upon their own persons." Confident in the efficacy of their sacred talisman, the Taira troops, at the battle of Yashima, in Sanuki, in 1185, placed this fan upon a pole in a boat, which was rowed to within fifty yards of the beach, in full view of the Genji, who were mockingly challenged to shoot at it. Nasu Munétaka, a Minamoto warrior, accepted the challenge, shot, and struck the fan, upon which the hostile army were greatly dismayed. In memory of this feat, Munétaka's descendants, the Sataké family, till lately lords of the castle-town of Akita, in Déwa, adopted for their badge a fan marked with a ball. They, however, "differenced" this device by changing the colours of their chief badge to a black ball on a white fan, their 3rd badge shewing a white ball on a black fan. We next meet with the *hi-no-maru* at the time of the invasion of Kiushiu by the Mongols in 1281. Whilst the Kamakura Shôgun, Koréyasu, was collecting forces to march against the enemy, he sent on, as leader of the vanguard, Utsunomiya Sadatsuna, to whom he gave two sacred banners, on which were portrayed respectively the sun and the moon. Both these devices were inscribed with the names of Buddhist deities. Upon Sadatsuna's arriving on the sea-coast at the scene of action, he unfurled these banners, when a sudden whirlwind arose and destroyed the Mongol fleet. The two flags were bestowed upon Sadatsuna as a reward, and were by him presented to the temple of Minobusan in Shinshiu. Subsequently the one marked with the sun (*hi-no-maru*) was transported to Saikiyôji, a temple near the village of Kamédo, close to Yedo, while the moon banner (*tsuki-no-maru*) was left in its original place. The banner brought to Saikiyôji is described in the " Yedo Meisho" as being $6\frac{1}{2}$ feet (Japanese) in length by $5\frac{1}{2}$ in breadth. Around the edges were marked eight dragons, within which, again, were portrayed the " Four Tennô" (four Buddhist guardian deities), while in the very centre was the *hi-no-maru* inscribed with the names of other Buddhist deities. A banner of this description is styled *hata mandara*. It was suspended, like the ordinary *hata* above-mentioned, from a crossbar fastened to a staff. Of late years, it may be remarked in passing, this word *hata* has been used in a much wider sense, and is the name at present given to *all* flags or banners, of no matter what shape. The suit of armour worn by Toyotomi Hidéyoshi, better known to foreigners as Taikô sama, (b. 1540—d. 1598), now on view at the *Hakubutsu-ku'an*, also bears the *hi-no-maru* in three places, namely, on the breastplate, and on the two shoulder-flaps. In this connection, it is interesting to note that on the Taikô's breastplate and gauntlets there are marked no less than eleven different badges, amongst others the Imperial *kiri* and *kiku*. From the above may be learned the antiquity of the present national device of Japan.

Nearly every public department in Japan now possesses its own special flag. That of the Board of Works bears the Chinese character *ko*, 工, (" works") in red on a white ground, and that of the Survey Department is divided diagonally from right to left, red and white, with the same character, in black, at the base. The War Department uses a white flag with the *hi-no-maru* adorned with 16 red rays, and the Marine Department a deeply indented horizontal red line, surmounted by an anchor of the same colour, the whole on a white ground. It will be observed that in every instance the Imperial colours of Japan, red and white, are strictly preserved.

So much importance has always been attached to flags by the Japanese, that we find the Christians who revolted at Shimabara in 1639, adopted and used as their war ensign a white flag marked with a red cross, as narrated in the " Shimabara-ki," a history of the revolt in question. So hateful in the eyes of the Japanese was this Christian symbol that in 1673, at Nagasaki, the crew of an English vessel named the " Return " were advised not to hoist the English flag with the cross of St. George. Fraissinet, who mentions this circumstance in his work " Le Japon," further quotes a passage from the journal of the voyage of the " Return," in which it is stated that a special flag had been made, *without the cross*, in order not to give offence to the prejudices of the Japanese, who took the cross to be a distinguishing mark of the Portuguese who had been expelled the country some 30 years previously. On one occasion, we are told, there was hoisted by mistake the flag containing the cross, and this was at once detected by the Japanese authorities, who sent off to enquire the reason. This little incident shows clearly what attention was paid in early days at Nagasaki to even so small a matter as a change in a Heraldic device. The cross does not hold here the honourable position that Western Heralds give to it ; it is exceedingly rare as a Japanese badge, and amongst the many suits of armour at the *Hakubutsu-ku'an* there is but one bearing this device,—as a Crest, on a small circular piece of metal.

Before leaving the heading of flags, it will not do to leave unmentioned that of the Mitsu Bishi Company, the Japanese Mail Steamship Company running between China and Japan. This well-known flag displays the device of three red diamonds, conjoined in the centre, on a white ground, thus bearing a " canting " allusion to the name of the Company. The diamond-shaped figures are

said to represent the seed-vessels of the water-plant called
hishi (the Water Caltrops) which is found in large
quantities in the province of Tosa, to which province belonged the merchants who started the Company. It is
not improbable that there is likewise contained an allusion
to the badge of the former *daimiô* of Tosa, the three oak-
leaves being "differenced" and changed into diamonds.

Of Monumental Heraldry there do not exist very strik-
ing examples. Indeed, with the exception of the devices
shown upon the mansions of the former *daimiôs*, hardly any
exist save those on tombstones. The badge is generally
sculptured in relief at the head of the stone, the inscription
coming immediately below it. In some instances it is
gilded. In temples, many of the *torii* or gateways are
ornamented with Heraldic devices carved upon them, and
in other places small plates of metal marked in similar
manner are affixed to the posts or beams of the buildings.
The tombs of the Tokugawa Shôguns at the temples at
Nikkô, in the province of Shimotsuké, and at Zôjôji, in
Yedo, furnish many beautifully executed specimens of
these devices.

In imitation of Foreign Orders of Knighthood, etc., the
Japanese Government, in February 1875, instituted an
"Order of Merit." This consists of eight classes, to each
of which is assigned its own peculiar decoration. The
decoration, in the case of the First Class, consists of an
eight-pointed star of thirty-two white enamelled rays, issuing from a red enamelled ball (the *hi-no-maru*) ; this is
worn on the right breast, while a badge consisting of a
smaller star of similar description, surmounted by a "five-
and seven *kiri*" in green and purple enamel, hangs from a
white ribbon with red edges worn across the right shoulder.
By the Second Class the star alone is worn, on the right
breast, while for the Third Class a narrow white and red
ribbon round the neck supports a smaller facsimile of the
badge of the First Class. Below the Third Class
the small badge only is worn, on the left breast, from
a small ribbon of the colours, and some difference is made
in the enamel and also in the number of flowers on the

kiri. The seventh and eighth classes wear the *kiri* only, without the irradiated *hi-no-maru* below it. The design is a good one, and the decoration compares very favourably with many of those seen in Europe. It would, perhaps, have had a better effect had the red ball in the centre been smaller, and surrounded by a circle of white enamel. This would not only have relieved the dark colour of the *hi-no-maru,* but would also have been in accordance with the strictest Heraldic usage, as showing likewise the *ground colour* of the national flag. A good precedent for this may be observed in the case of the star of the English order of the Garter, where the red cross of St. George has a narrow white edging, the better to represent the device of the English "White Ensign." The Japanese War Medal, which was likewise instituted in February 1875, is of silver, and hangs from a white ribbon edged with green, worn on the left breast. The obverse bears the Chinese characters for " War Medal," while the date is engraved on the reverse.

For the sake of pure Heraldic art in this country, it is to be regretted that several of the Japanese officials who have visited Europe have carried their imitation of foreign usages so far as to invent and make use of Supporters for their Badges. This arises from ignorance of the fact that in Heraldry it is only a *shield,* not a *badge* or *crest,* that can have supporters, and it should likewise not be forgotten that in the West it is only to persons of a certain rank that Heralds accord the right to bear supporters to their shields. But, in the absence of any definite rules of Heraldic art in Japan, these anomalies are likely to continue.

It does not, however, seen very probable that any perfect system of Heraldry will arise in this country. With the fall of the feudal régime passed away the most favourable opportunity for its establishment, as in the case also of the countries of the West. In Europe, Heraldry is at this date little more than an interesting study of the past, as a companion to Historical research ; and in Japan there does not appear any reason to hope for a revival of

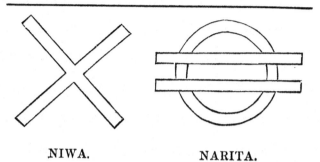

NIWA.   NARITA.

IMPERIAL *KIKU*.   IMPERIAL *KIRI*.

TOKUGAWA.   HONDA.

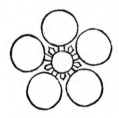

MAËDA.

SHIMADZU.

(1st.)—YAMANOUCHI.—(2nd.)

(1st.)—KURODA.—(2nd.)

HACHISUKA (2ND.)

THE FYLFOT.

(1ST.)—ARIMA.—(2ND.)

THE *TOMOYÉ*.

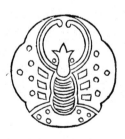

IKÉDA.—(1ST.)

 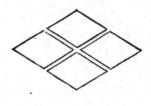

(1st.)—NAMBU.—(2nd.)

 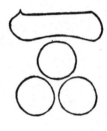

(1st.)—MÔRI.—(2nd.)

(1st.)—DATÉ.—(2nd.)

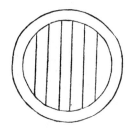

DATÉ (3RD.)

ASANO.

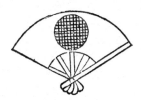

SATAKÉ.

KUSUNOKI.

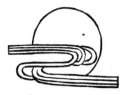

NAKAYAMA.

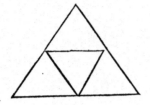 

HÔJÔ.   CHIBA NO TANÉMICHI.

CROSS CREST,
AT EXHIBITION DE-
PARTMENT.

MIDZUNO.   AÖKI.

FLAGS.

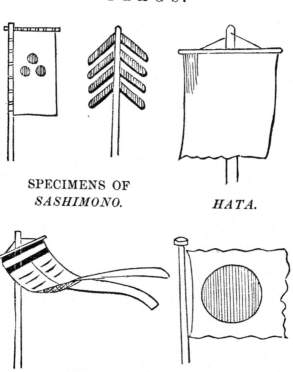

SPECIMENS OF
SASHIMONO.

HATA.

FUKI-NAGASHI.

NATIONAL FLAG.

OLD STANDARDS AT EXHIBITION
DEPARTMENT.

FLAGS.

BOARD OF WORKS.

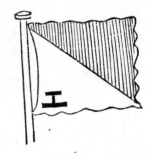

SURVEY DEPT.

WAR DEPT.

NAVAL DEPT.

MITSU BISHI Co.

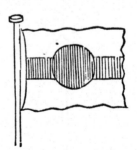

POST OFFICE.

MISCELLANEOUS.

MISCELLANEOUS.

MISCELLANEOUS.

MISCELLANEOUS.

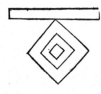  

an art which has long since seen its most palmy days in other lands. The above notes may, however, prove of some interest to any one who has studied Western Heraldry, and at least give rise to a comparison between the old system of our own middle ages, and that followed during the late feudal times of the Empire of Japan.

ASIATIC SOCIETY OF JAPAN.

A general meeting of the above society was held in the Imperial University *(Kai Sei Gakko)* on Wednesday, the 25th instant, Sir Harry Parkes, President, in the chair.

The minutes of the last annual meeting, as given in the new volume of the Transactions, were then read; also those of the Council meeting in which it was notified that Professor D. H. Marshall was appointed Recording Secretary for Tôkiô in place of Professor Summers, whose resignation was necessitated by his removal to Niigata.

These minutes having been approved of by the society, the names of three new members were announced, Professor Dixon, J. H. Longford, Esq., and Professor Milne.

Sir Harry Parkes then called upon Mr. McClatchie to read the paper for the evening—"Japanese Heraldry," which thereafter called for some very complimentary remarks from the President on the erudition in Japanese literature as well as knowledge of the science of Heraldry displayed in the paper. He thought that the crusades, tournaments, and wearing of shields and armour would account for the great advance Heraldry had made in the West in the middle ages. He did not know whether so much value was attached to pedigrees in the East as in the West, but if so we must look to China for very long pedigrees. Mr. McClatchie had said that Feudality was productive of Heraldry. China, like Japan, had her feudal system, but he did not remember seeing any Heraldry there. The figure called the *tomoye* was, he thought, probably derived from the Chinese figure, painted in black and white, standing for the origin of all things.

Dr. Geerts asked whether Mr. McClatchie was quite sure that the three leaves in the Tokugawa crest were holyhock, and that they were not three leaves of *Saishin* or *Hazarum Sieboldii*. Mr. McClatchie said that the Japanese name of these leaves in the badge was certainly the holyhock.

Professor Ayrton thought that different members of the same family, having different badges, might be parallel to the custom of some English families whose members adopted different mottoes although the same crest. He observed that it apparently was the modern fashion to wear three *mons* instead of five on the *haori*, one on the back and one on each sleeve. Mr. Ayrton also thought that the study of badges lead to the study of shop signs. The well-known sign of the bush outside a *saké* shop is the same as that used in England, which gave rise to the proverb "Good wine needs no bush."

Dr. Faulds, remarking on the doubt whether the Mikado's crest represented the sun or the crysanthemum, suggested that it might represent the sunflower, which certainly is seen growing in Japan now, but whether or not it did formerly he did not know.

In answer to one remark of Sir H. Parkes', Mr. McClatchie observed regarding Heraldry in China, that he had noticed that at the change of guards at the gates of cities, each commander had his own special standard.

The meeting was then brought to a close.

rmation can be obtained
Gtesting.com
e USA
452150217
LV00027B/900/P

CPSIA inf
at www.IC
Printed in t
LVOW13s
524370